UNDYING LOVE

Tears of Gold

RICKY JONES JR.

authorHOUSE®

AuthorHouse™
1663 Liberty Drive
Bloomington, IN 47403
www.authorhouse.com
Phone: 1 (800) 839-8640

Published by AuthorHouse   01/09/2018

ISBN: 978-1-5462-2393-1 (sc)
ISBN: 978-1-5462-2392-4 (e)

Library of Congress Control Number: 2018900181

Print information available on the last page.

This book is printed on acid-free paper.

I miss you

Gold leaves floating in the air,
Touching my face,
Memories of you come to mind,
The moments we shared,
The love we created,
The everlasting friendship,
Still mourning the loss of you,
I will always hold on to you,
Your spirit hugs my broken heart,
I will always love you,
No one will ever replace you,
Forever my soul mate,
We will meet again,
Two angels reunited,
Flying over the stars of heaven,
Hand in Hand,
Heart to Heart,
We are as one,
I miss you my love,
But you will always live in my heart,
Keeping me warm inside,
Until we meet again,
Loving you always.

Crossing Over

My soul has left the human body,
I am crossing over,
Entering the new world,
I have no fear,
I welcome happiness,
There's a beginning,
There's an ending,
Enjoy every moment of your life,
Each day is a true blessing,
Nothing is promised,
The past is gone,
All the pain and suffering is still sometimes felt,
I learned many lessons along the way though,
Reflecting on my broken heart,
Reflecting on my failed relationships,
Some of which were never worth my time,
All the tears gave me strength to change and move on,
Material possessions were never my ultimate goal,
Getting closer to God and creating my own happiness was my goal,
Being a kind person,
Treating people with love and respect,
Never judging others as I wouldn't want to be,
Embracing the storms and finally walking across the rainbow,
Crossing over,
Seeing God's face,
Truly happy.

The Temple

My body is a temple,
Built from the ground up,
A place of peace,
A place of hope,
A place of worship,
Cleansing myself of poison and negativity,
Worshipping my lord and savior,
Being grateful for everything that I have,
Many storms have come and gone,
Trying to destroy the foundation that I've built,
But I'm still standing,
Strong and powerful,
Beautiful and loving,
Conquering my greatest fears,
My temple will not be destroyed.

Forever Yours

Staring into your eyes,
I see a dream about to come true,
Our love,
Our life,
Our wedding,
All coming together,
Connected in a bond that no one could ever break,
Holding your hand,
Carrying your heart,
Flying with your spirit,
We are both protected,
A shield of true love,
Able to go against the storm,
Growing stronger every season,
I am forever yours,
My heart is melting,
My soul is blossoming,
My spirit has reached the stars of heaven,
Blessing us with an undeniable love,
I love you,
Now and always,
You are forever mine,
I am forever yours.

Tranquil Beauty

Broken pieces of gold,
Leading me to true happiness,
Surrounded by crystal blue waters,
Baptizing my soul and spirit,
I am renewed,
I am reborn,
A brand new person,
Peace now enters my heart,
Mending my broken soul,
White roses flourishing in tranquil beauty,
I am no longer broken,
I am complete,
Expressing my heart to God,
Asking for true forgiveness,
Releasing the poison and regret from my body,
I now look forward,
Never backwards,
You can't change the past,
But you can create your own future,
Those beautiful white roses,
Purifying my spirit,
Opening my heart to full blossom,
I can now smile again once more.

Breaking Free

My spirit has left the human body,
Breaking into the sunlight,
Feeling God's warm embrace,
All the negativity,
All the poison,
All the scars have left my body,
A beautiful spirit colliding with the stars,
No more tears,
No more regret,
No more sorrow,
I am breaking free,
No looking back,
The next life begins,
Destiny has been revealed,
God carries my golden heart into his kingdom,
My everlasting smile is shown,
Ivory wings flying me into eternal beauty,
I am breaking free.

Sad Eyes-(Journey of an angel)

Beauty died inside of me a long time ago,
But came back after many seasons,
The angel with the frozen heart,
Consumed with bitterness for many years,
Going through many trials,
Shedding so many tears,
Lies,
Regret,
Anger,
Shame,
Bitter elements circling around my life,
Not knowing if happiness would enter my heart,
A part of me wants to live,
A part of me wants to die,
I am in deep mourning over the past,
Events that have changed my life forever,
Pieces of my soul drown into the sea,
My tears are very real,
The pain is deeply felt,
Enduring the storms,
Surviving the bitter seasons,
My sad eyes reveal everything,
Still beauty comes out of the darkness,
I will smile again,
Continuing my journey,
Walking along the golden road,
Holding God's hand,
Reaching my destiny,
Journey of an angel.

Stars of hope

Golden stars carry my heart to heaven,
Every broken piece has come back together,
The tears,
The heartache,
The regret,
All melting away,
I have always held on to hope,
My absolute faith in God,
Angels renew my broken heart,
Making me believe in love again,
I have already found my soul mate,
Journey of gold,
Journey of darkness,
Journey of tears,
God carries my soul through the turbulent storms,
Bringing me through some of the most difficult times of my life,
I will be forever grateful,
Stars of hope,
Stars of heaven,
Stars of God,
Never losing faith,
Never losing hope,
Never forgetting what really matters in life,
My family,
My heart,
My destiny,
Stars of hope.

The Next Life

Born to live,
Born to die,
This world gets colder each day,
So much racism,
So much injustice,
So much hate,
Bringing my eyes to deep tears,
Drowning my heart in sorrow,
Voices crying,
Voices unheard,
Voices lost,
We are all human beings,
No matter what color our skin is,
No matter what our sexual orientation is,
We all cry,
We all bleed,
We all die,
Maybe in the next life,
Hearts will open,
Souls will heal,
Hate will disappear,
We need change,
We need kind hearts,
We need compassion,
Hate is never the answer,
Erase the ignorant hatred from your mind and heart,
Embrace the gift of God,
Love,
The next life.

One sweet day

One sweet day,
My golden wings will take me away from this tragic earth,
My sad eyes will disappear,
Every regret will fade away,
My soul will be transformed into everlasting beauty,
Broken pieces of my heart will come together,
Bonding,
Healing,
Renewing,
One sweet day,
I will wake up with a big smile,
Seeing all my past loved ones again,
Hugging my grandmother,
Enjoying the precious moments that matter,
The pain is gone,
The sadness is gone,
I embrace God's true blessing,
Learning so much through the years,
Surviving the turbulent storms,
Remembering every tear,
Praying for peace in my heart and spirit,
I know my purpose,
I know my fate,
I accept it,
I embrace it,
One sweet day.

Autumn Leaves

Seasons change,
People change,
But my heart will always belong to you,
You are a beautiful memory,
Always on my mind,
Always in my heart,
You blossom under God's ray of light,
With our love growing stronger everyday,
Seasons come and go,
But my love for you will always remain,
Autumn leaves,
So golden,
So real,
Falling from the sky,
Bonding our souls together,
We both shed tears,
Happiness has finally come for us,
Walking down the golden road,
No longer broken,
No longer fragile,
Stronger than ever,
Autumn leaves,
Loving you more every season,
Every kiss,
Every touch,
Every moment,
At last.

Human Being

I have lied,
I have cheated,
I have manipulated,
Never proud of my past actions,
I am a human being,
But I will never use that as an excuse,
A broken man,
A broken heart,
Full of hurt and resentment,
Nearly poisoning half of my life,
I cry,
I bleed,
I ask for forgiveness,
Praying to God to rejuvenate my spirit,
Every tear leaves a bittersweet memory,
Memories that will always be a part of me,
I am a human being,
Living,
Learning,
Growing,
Mourning,
I still carry these sad brown eyes,
But my story still continues,
I hope that I will have a beautiful ending.

Our Love

Since day one,
I loved you,
With everything in my heart,
Our love,
Our bond,
Our spirit,
Forever beautiful,
No storm could ever tear us apart,
No disease,
No sickness,
No person,
You are my beautiful friend,
Loved unconditionally,
We are two golden angels,
Hand in Hand,
Rising above the stars and into heaven,
With our hearts melting into one,
True love,
True joy,
True heart,
This is real love,
Until my life ends,
Until your life ends,
We will always love each other,
Love is beautiful,
Love is precious,
Love is ours,
Forever.

Golden Halo

Walking up the stairs of heaven,
My heart is at true peace,
My eyes are weeping tears of joy,
I have finally made it,
Leaving the darkness and evil behind,
Embracing God's beautiful heart,
Transforming me into an amazing spirit,
Soaring through the clouds,
Soaring through the stars,
Melting into heaven,
I now wear the golden halo,
All the negativity,
All the poison,
All the pain,
Finally leaving my body,
I am pure,
I am clean,
I am whole,
A beautiful angel,
Forgiven for my past sins,
Accepted for who I am,
Loved as a true human being,
My golden halo,
Shining forever,
Heaven sent.

Making Love

Lonely heart,
Broken with tears,
Not knowing if I would ever find true love,
Until one day,
A stranger enters my life and changes it forever,
Beautiful smile,
Humble eyes,
Loving spirit,
I was quite smitten,
A loving friendship begins,
Holding hands,
Deep conversation,
A true understanding of each other,
Didn't think I would meet anyone so special,
Two broken spirits colliding with each other,
Love has grown in my garden,
Despite the many storms that have come and gone,
We still grow,
We still blossom,
We are still in love,
Making love,
A true essence of our unity.

Beautiful Morning

God's ray shines on my heart,
Blooming into eternity,
I am blessed to be alive,
A beautiful morning,
My eyes are wide open,
No longer full of tears,
Only peace and joy enters this spirit,
Being grateful for the heart that God has blessed me with,
I deeply reflect,
My life,
My soul,
My love,
Losing and gaining,
Failing and achieving,
Grieving and moving on,
A beautiful morning,
Angels whisper in my ears,
A lovely melody embraces my heart,
I am carefree,
I am loving,
I am free,
A beautiful morning.

Moon Glow

Angels in the night,
Whispering to my spirit,
I slowly die into the dark clouds of heaven,
My soul floats into the midnight air,
Embracing every beautiful star in the sky,
I am no longer in pain,
No longer broken,
No longer in heartache,
Crisp cool air wraps around my spirit,
Frozen in time,
Remembering the moment when I was truly happy,
The beauty,
The excitement,
The journey,
Never forgotten.

Moonlight

Beautiful stars fall upon my face,
Revealing the beauty that died so long ago,
Erasing the bitterness,
Erasing the darkness,
Erasing the resentment,
God's ray of light shines down on me,
Melting the heart of frozen tears,
Revealing the true happiness buried deep inside,
Past events broke my heart into a million pieces,
Not knowing if I would ever smile again,
Mourning in silence for years,
One night I revealed my true heart to God,
God revealed the moonlight of heaven to me,
With golden stars pouring down on me,
Melting away the mask that covered my face for so long,
True beauty has returned,
The painful tears are starting to fade,
A smile finally emerges,
I have survived the battlefield of love and life,
The moonlight,
So rare and beautiful,
Following my spirit in the midnight sky,
Both colliding,
Angel of mercy,
Angel of death,
Angel of love,
I am finally happy.

Fading Star

I wish I could fade away,
Fade away into the crystal blue sky,
Never to be seen or heard from again,
The only reminder of me would be my golden heart drowning into the
ocean,
The love,
The kindness,
The memories,
My only legacy,
I am the fading star,
With a heart that outshines any hatred thrown at me,
A cruel world we live in,
A world of bigots,
A world of hate,
Very sad indeed,
Who would want to live in a world like this?
This is not the world that I used to know,
I am the angel of broken wings,
A fading star of heaven,
One day my wings will be mended,
I will enter the gates of heaven once more,
Fading into the wind,
Fading out of life,
Leaving my beautiful heart,
The only reminder of my existence.

Pearls of wisdom

My tears,
My heart,
My spirit,
All sacred to me,
I have learned so many lessons,
Love and life,
Friends and enemies,
Life and death,
Deep sacrifices of the heart and mind,
Growing stronger each day,
Hurtful tears turning into black pearls,
Pearls of wisdom,
Life is beautiful,
Life is tragic,
Life is wisdom,
The broken road turns into beautiful gold,
Angels are walking by my side,
Protecting me from harm,
Leading me into destiny,
These beautiful black pearls,
Buried deep in my heart forever,
Knowledge is power,
Wisdom is my greatest treasure.

Day of Mourning

My heart burning into ashes,
The love has died,
The spirit is gone,
Day of mourning,
The past comes back to haunt me,
Reminding me of the deep hurt I once felt,
The people who hurt me,
The betrayal I felt,
The tears that I've shed for many years,
I cannot look back anymore,
Open wounds have healed but the scar still remains,
Always a reminder,
Always a feeling,
Always in my heart,
My day of mourning is over,
A new day,
A new time,
A new dream,
My heart is reborn,
Gold petals rise from the burning ashes,
Eyes filled with tears of happiness,
I am a survivor,
With each day making me stronger,
Leaving the past far behind,
I look ahead,
Following the rainbow,
A new dream,
A new memory,
A new heart.

Loving You

My sweetheart,
My love,
My soul mate,
I will always love you,
Whether we are together or apart,
The bond will always be there,
The magic will never disappear,
Our love is forever,
Until the end of time,
Until the end of my life,
I will be loving you,
Beauty has sewn our hearts together,
Two spirits glowing,
Two spirits soaring through the clouds,
Two spirits in love,
No storm will ever come between us,
God's rainbow will guide us to happiness,
Now and always,
Loving you.

Dream Come True

My heart was cold and black,
Full of hurt and regret,
Until I met you,
The only person to open my broken heart,
Your smile,
Your presence,
Your spirit,
My dream come true,
Never knew what real was until I met you,
Soul mate,
Dreamlover,
Best friend,
Connecting in every element,
My heart is now open,
Full of beautiful roses,
Blooming forever into eternity,
True love created,
Season of tears are finally over,
No longer weeping in sorrow,
Happiness enters my body,
Creating a feeling like no other,
You are my dream come true,
Entering my life,
Forever changed,
My beautiful love.

Journey to God

A heart swept away in tears,
Enduring the stillness of bitter gold,
Broken pieces of my heart scattered everywhere,
Each piece brings a memory,
Each piece brings hope,
Making me stronger and wiser,
The hurt,
The agony,
The pain,
Never knowing if those raw emotions would ever heal,
With bitterness comes beauty,
I continue on this journey,
Trying to reach the golden rainbow,
The rainbow of God and his angels,
I am not perfect,
I have sinned,
I have lied,
I have cheated,
But I have also learned,
Never to be a hypocrite,
Never to judge,
Never to let the past trap you into misery,
My heart is baptized in the blue waters of heaven,
My soul rises from the burned ashes of life,
My spirit glows from the sunlight of God's power,
I am almost there,
Reaching for God's hand,
I am safe,
I am loved,
I am forgiven,
Journey to God.

Tragic Kingdom

This cruel world,
Crumbling right in front of me,
People losing faith,
People losing hope,
Hearts fading into black ashes,
A tragic kingdom,
Breaking my heart everyday,
Small pieces of beauty still try to linger on,
A part of me seems to die within these storms,
The world that I used to know,
A world that I used to love,
Fading in front of my eyes,
A tragic kingdom.

Remember Me

The first time I kissed you,
The first time I held you in my arms,
So magical,
So beautiful,
So romantic,
The first time I made love to you,
Our bond,
Our love,
Our ecstasy,
All so real,
The moment,
The reality,
The tears,
Our broken hearts drowning in sorrow,
Missing you,
Loving you,
Yearning for you,
I want you to remember,
Remember the beauty,
Remember the love,
Remember our neverending story,
Remember me,
I will always love you.

Beyond Beauty

My kindness,
My love,
My heart,
Look beyond the beauty,
Look beyond my appearance,
Look inside my heart and soul,
A human being stands there,
There is so much more beyond my looks,
Empathy,
Compassion,
Forgiveness,
The three elements of my being,
Love me for who I truly am,
Love me for my inner beauty,
Love me unconditionally,
Beyond the mask,
Beyond the illusion,
Beyond the beauty.

Lavender Dream-(Dedicated to Betty Guest)

Your face,
Your smile,
Your hugs,
Frozen forever in my heart,
Never melting,
Never forgotten,
Dear grandmother,
You are my lavender dream,
An essence of pure beauty,
Always thinking of you,
Missing you,
Beautiful tears still shed for you grandma,
I hope that you are well,
I hope that you are safe and happy,
Angel of heaven,
Angel of my heart,
I hope to join you one day,
That day will truly be my happiness,
I feel your spirit,
I feel your embrace,
I feel protected,
You are my lavender dream,
I love you grandma.

Let me live

I am my own person,
I am my own self,
I am not a robot,
You will not use me,
You will not control me,
You will not manipulate me,
Let me live,
Let me breathe,
Let me go,
Accept me for who I am,
Accept the truth,
Accept my way of life,
No more lies,
No more mask,
No more hiding,
This is the real me,
Let me live.

The greatest love

Two angels,
Two hearts,
One true love,
I feel your love,
I feel your spirit,
I live inside of your heart,
You live inside of my heart,
Beautiful spirits bound,
Through the rain,
Through the storms,
Through the heartache,
We remain together,
With every tear giving us strength,
My soul mate,
My beauty,
My love,
Always you,
We continue on this journey,
It never ends,
Even after our lives are over on this earth,
Our spirits will remain forever bonded,
Two angels rising up above the stars of heaven,
The greatest love.

Compassion

Your tears,
Your heart,
Your soul,
Blend into a beautiful melody,
The suffering,
The love,
The loss,
I feel it deep inside me,
We are both angels,
Living in a tragic kingdom,
Walking a bittersweet journey,
Despite the hurt,
I hold you,
I hug you,
I love you,
Deep compassion covers my broken heart,
Forgiveness is shown,
The coldness in my soul has melted,
You will always be,
The one that I cherish,
The one that I dream about,
The one that I love,
Always you.

Angel Song-(My love for you)

Our love is a symphony,
A melody of heaven,
So beautiful,
So touching,
So real,
Two angels soaring through the clouds,
With our wings flowing so gently,
My love for you goes beyond this life,
I cherish,
I adore,
I love,
The moments we share,
The love that we create,
A rare feeling that I never felt before,
Tears shed from my heart to yours,
Bonding us through the years,
Many storms have passed us,
But God's rainbow has kept us together,
A season of change,
A season of hope,
A season of dreams,
Our true angel song,
My soul mate,
My heart,
My life,
You are my everything,
My love for you.

Peace of Mind

My heart is buried in a blanket of soft snow,
Raw emotions have been controlling my life for so long,
A beautiful spirit fading in the wind,
A heart broken on the journey of love and life,
Tears streaming down my face,
I pray to the angels of the heavenly skies,
I pray to my Lord and savior,
God's hand calms my torn spirit,
My heart is at peace,
Floating on air and into eternity,
All the worry,
All the stress,
All the heartache,
Disappearing before my eyes,
My love is strong,
My faith is solid,
My journey is not over yet,
God continues to lead the way,
I am surrounded with joy and serenity,
A heart no longer buried,
The snow has melted,
A new season begins,
With a heart that blossoms into the sun,
I have a peace of mind.

Darkness

A heart cold as ice,
A heart dark as night,
A heart dying slowly,
My emotions are raw,
Strong and deep,
Killing me slowly,
But faith is not lost,
Hope is not gone,
God's beautiful light reaches out to me,
Healing my broken heart,
Sewing my torn spirit back together,
Melting away the ice that was frozen in my body,
I want to release,
I want to let go,
I want to bloom again,
The darkness slowly starts to fade,
My journey is set,
My purpose is shown,
My love is glowing ,
The darkness is gone.

Always You

The one that I think about,
The one that I dream about,
The one that I will always love,
My true heart,
My true partner,
My soul mate,
Seasons have come and gone,
Storms have rained upon us,
But the love we share always survived,
God's beautiful rainbow bonds us together,
With vivid beauty shining through,
Our spirits connecting together,
Soaring through the clouds of heaven,
Hand in hand,
Heart to heart,
We are forever,
We are loving,
We are beautiful,
Always in love,
Always in deep,
Always you.

On my way

Weeping tears of happiness,
Flowing on my golden wings,
I am on my way,
To embrace God's love,
To embrace his beautiful heart,
To ask for his forgiveness,
I am a broken man,
I am a broken soul,
Trying to put the pieces of my life back together,
Each day I get stronger,
Each day I become wiser,
Each day my heart heals,
Memories of the past try to haunt me,
But I hold on to my faith,
I hold on to God's spirit,
Letting the open wounds heal on their own time,
The bleeding will stop,
The hurt will stop,
True happiness does exist,
I am on my way,
To the golden road,
To my true destiny,
To my fate,
I am on my way.

Precious Dove

Beautiful blue lake,
Surrounded with peace and serenity,
Floating with precious white doves,
I am walking alone,
I am in deep thought,
But my heart is free and pure,
Toxic poison has finally left,
Feeling like an angel,
A floating spirit of heaven,
Precious doves circle around me,
Spreading their wings,
Releasing the emotion,
Releasing the beauty,
Releasing the love,
I step into the crystal blue waters,
Melting into eternity,
Leaving this tragic kingdom behind,
Entering a new world,
The journey continues,
Never ends.

Wings of Glory

My beautiful golden wings,
Shielding me from evil,
I am strong,
I am brave,
I am fearless,
Reaching the throne of God,
Asking for his love,
Asking for his forgiveness,
I am forever baptized in the sacred waters of heaven,
Cleansing my spirit,
Cleansing my soul,
Opening my heart,
Nothing or no one will keep me from my God,
No judgement,
No doubt,
No hatred,
I will reach my destination,
My wings of glory will carry me home,
I will be loved,
I will be accepted,
I am the angel of heaven,
Forever love,
Forever beauty,
The glory of God.

Journey to my heart

Come with me,
Hold my hand,
Hold on tight,
I will keep you safe,
Trust me,
Trust my spirit,
Follow your destiny,
Journey to my heart,
My love for you is quite clear,
The smiles,
The laughter,
The essence,
Not a dream,
Not an illusion,
This is the real thing,
Let me hug you,
Let me guide you,
Wrap you around my beautiful heart,
I will love you,
I will protect you,
I will cherish you,
Now and forever,
Follow the golden road,
Follow the journey,
Journey to my heart.

Beautiful tears

Flowing into my heart,
Pouring into my soul,
Melting into the sunset,
Beautiful tears,
God's rainbow will always connect us,
Your eyes,
Your smile,
Your spirit,
Treasured forever in my life,
The joy,
The memories,
The love,
Cherished always,
Our journey still continues,
Always golden,
Always beautiful,
Our tears will guide us home,
The pain,
The sorrow,
The healing,
Forever buried in my heart,
Drowning in a sea of beautiful tears,
A new life begins,
The spirit of you,
The spirit of us,
Always golden.

Heart of roses

Under the sky,
Under the sun,
Under the stars,
My heart blooms endlessly,
Full of love,
Full of harmony,
Surviving the cold winter of earth,
A cruel society,
A cruel world,
Each day becomes a test,
Every moment truly matters,
Despite the hurt,
Despite the hate,
My heart will always remain beautiful,
Sometimes broken,
Full of tears,
Mourning the tragic memories of the past,
But God's rainbow always heals my spirit,
My heart is buried in a garden of roses,
Blooming forever,
This beauty,
This dream,
This moment,
Always forever,
This kind of love will never die.

Hand in hand

Together we walk on the golden road,
Hand in hand,
Heart to heart,
We are bonded forever,
Memories keep our love alive,
Storms bring tears to my eyes,
But together we remain strong,
Our love is rare,
Our love is beautiful,
Our love is forever,
After this life,
After this death,
The love will always remain,
Two golden stars reunited in the skies of heaven,
You and I,
Hand in hand.

Rainbow of promise

My heart is pure,
My spirit is golden,
My faith is strong,
With God's heart surrounding me,
I am emotional with fear,
Revealing my true self,
No lies,
No deception,
No mask,
God sees all,
I ask for kindness,
I ask for forgiveness,
I ask for the keys to God's kingdom,
Crying on God's shoulder,
He holds me tight,
Wiping away my tears,
I look up at the sky,
He reveals the rainbow of promise,
The promise to love and forgive the brokenhearted,
The promise to renew my soul and spirit,
A beautiful rainbow wrapped around my torn heart,
Sowing the seeds of love back into it,
I embrace,
I love,
I cherish,
God's rainbow of promise.

Forever Heart

We share a love,
We share a heart,
We share a life,
True friends,
True soul mates,
True magic,
Going through a journey of laughter and tears,
Our love brought us closer together,
The love that I carry in my heart for you,
I will never have that with anyone else,
A beautiful bond of two strangers that fell in love,
Our life is a story book,
A different chapter,
A different season,
A bittersweet ending,
But our love will never be over,
We are two angels,
With our wings floating together in the sky,
My tears in your heart,
Your tears in mine,
We were meant to be,
The person that I love,
The person that I cherish,
You will always be,
Forever in my heart.

Thorns of life

My life is a beautiful rose,
Full of thorns,
Full of emotion,
Every touch leaves bitter blood behind,
Everything is not quite as it seems,
I carry sad eyes,
I carry a broken heart,
Tragic memories refuse to let my spirit go,
I live a bittersweet life,
A few smiles,
A few laughs,
But not truly happy,
At least not yet,
Dreams broken,
Memories fading in the wind,
This is not the world that I used to know,
People full of hate,
Carrying hearts with black holes,
Blinded with such ignorance and bigotry,
I know that God loves and accepts me,
I refuse to wear a fake mask all of my life,
Stay true to yourself,
Living a lie is not the answer,
Sometimes I hate this world,
I would love to just fly away to a new world and never return,
Some days I feel like broken glass,
Not knowing if those broken pieces will ever come back together,
My heart,
My soul,
My destiny,
All tied to a beautiful rose.

Free spirit

Soaring through the clouds,
Touching every beautiful star,
Staring into the kingdom of heaven,
I am a free spirit,
Walking on a bittersweet journey,
Enjoying the rain that follows me,
I learn,
I grow,
I move on,
Falling in love,
Falling out of love,
Leaving behind the tears that made me grow,
Leaving behind the people that left scars on my body,
My spirit continues to flow,
My heart blossoms everyday,
Grateful for the blessings of the Lord,
Living,
Breathing,
Exploring,
I am a free spirit,
Enjoying every single moment of my life,
The tears will fade,
The scars will heal,
My spirit will live on forever.

Weeping heart

My life is an open book,
My heart is an open rosebud,
But sometimes the rosebud dies in the cold season,
Tears of life,
Tears of joy,
Tears of sorrow,
My weeping heart,
Flooding the depths of my soul,
Cleansing the darkness of my spirit,
I am a torn man,
I have regrets,
I have memories,
I have deep emotions buried inside of me,
My smile is a disguise,
Covering the sadness that lies within me,
No one will ever truly understand where I'm coming from,
Some have walked my path,
Some have never been on my journey,
Follow the trail of tears and you will understand more clearly,
The beauty,
The darkness,
The reality,
Accepting the things that I cannot change,
Making peace with God in my heart and spirit,
Transforming into that beautiful angel of earth,
My weeping heart.

The Loner-(Walking Away)

The liars,
The cheaters,
The phonies,
I am walking away,
I am the loner,
I am following my own path,
Beautiful soul,
Beautiful heart,
Golden spirit,
Never to be changed,
Never to be tarnished,
Never to be destroyed,
My circle is quite clear,
No negativity,
No hate,
No judgements,
I will not walk on eggshells for anyone,
I will speak my mind,
I will speak the truth,
Accept it,
Embrace it,
Cherish it,
I am the loner,
Walking away from evil,
Walking into my destiny.

Legacy

Beautiful ashes flowing,
Melodies of my heart playing,
My spirit is flowing and free,
Always cherish,
Always remember,
My legacy,
Human kindness,
True humanity,
A pure heart of gold,
I am the loner with a heart of roses,
Blooming forever until the end of my life,
This is a cold world,
This is a sad world,
Full of racism and hate,
Which I will never understand,
Warm tears melt away the bitter heart I had for so long,
I refuse to hate,
I refuse to stay bitter,
I will not be defeated,
God's rainbow wraps around my beautiful spirit,
Until the end,
I will be remembered,
A beautiful poet with an amazing heart,
Loving and giving,
Touching the hearts of the sad and lonely,
Expressing my love to the angels that are walking on earth,
My faith,
My journey,
My legacy,
Always remembered,
Never forgotten.

Undying Love-(Tears of Gold)

Taking my last breath,
I hold on to your hand,
Never wanting to let go,
Staring into those beautiful eyes,
Knowing that my spirit is about to fly away into heaven,
I love you so much,
Always know and remember the love that I carry for you,
Endless,
Timeless,
Sacred,
Forever and always,
My sweetheart,
My best friend,
With a bond that was always golden,
Undying love,
My wings will always protect you,
Shielding you from harm,
Never leaving you,
In heart,
In spirit,
I will be here,
You are crying the tears of gold,
Spreading all over my heart,
Awakening the beautiful soul that was buried for so long,
I thank you,
My soul mate,
My dear one,
I am leaving this earth but I am not leaving you,
My heart will always be in your hands,
My soul will always surround you,
Our tears of gold will bond us forever.

A Significant Life

I know my purpose,
I know my heart,
I understand so many things now,
My lover and best friend almost died,
My heart was drowning in tears,
Seeing him in the hospital connected to so many machines,
Truly broke my heart,
Not knowing if this ugly storm would ever go away,
He opened his eyes and saw my face,
He started to smile and cry,
I gave him the will to live and keep going,
When everything seemed like it was going to end,
I prayed,
I kept my faith,
I stayed by his side,
I never left him,
My heart was always connected to his beautiful spirit,
My purpose became so much more clear,
Human kindness is the greatest gift that you can give someone,
Never lose yourself to this superficial world,
Never lose the true person that you are,
Anyone can easily fall into a black hole and lose themselves forever,
My purpose in this life is to give kindness and love to the broken angels who
have been forgotten,
No matter who you are,
No matter what disease you have,
You are a human being,
Deserving to be treated with kindness and respect from everyone,
No amount of money can bring the dead back to life,
Cherish what you have and who you have because life is short.

Printed in the United States
By Bookmasters